Rocks, Wind, and Water

By Jeri Cipriano

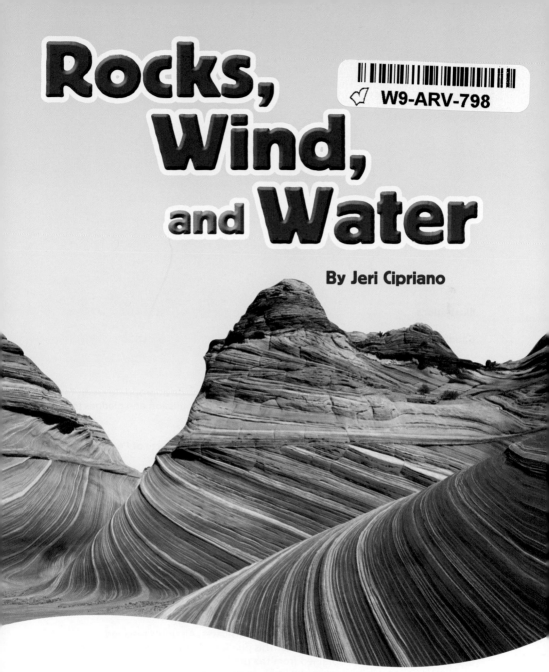

Scott Foresman
is an imprint of

Glenview, Illinois • Boston, Massachusetts • Chandler, Arizona •
Upper Saddle River, New Jersey

Illustrations

6 Judith Hunt.

Photographs

Every effort has been made to secure permission and provide appropriate credit for photographic material. The publisher deeply regrets any omission and pledges to correct errors called to its attention in subsequent editions.

Unless otherwise acknowledged, all photographs are the property of Pearson Education, Inc.

Photo locators denoted as follows: Top (T), Center (C), Bottom (B), Left (L), Right (R), Background (Bkgd)

Opener: ©Stockxpert; **1** ©Tom Bean/Corbis; **3** ©Demetrio Carrasco/©DK Images; **4** SCPhotos/Alamy Images; **5** Jupiter Images; **7** ©Stockxpert; **8** ©Tom Bean/Corbis; **10** ©David Wall/Alamy Images; **11** ©David M Dennis/Oxford Science/PhotoLibrary Group, Inc.; **12** ©Stockxpert.

ISBN 13: 978-0-328-46913-0
ISBN 10:   0-328-46913-0

3 4 5 6 7 8 9 10 V010 13 12 11 10

This is the Grand Canyon. It's about one mile deep. You can look down from the top and see layers of rocks in its walls. Far, far below you'll see a river.

Take a mule ride down into the Grand Canyon. You'll pass the layers of rocks. The lower you go, the older the rocks are. The rocks at the bottom are two billion years old!

The Colorado River flows at the bottom of the Grand Canyon. The river made the canyon. How did this happen?

Let's go back about six million years. Back then, there was no Grand Canyon. The river flowed through a plain. So where did the canyon come from?

It took millions of years to make the canyon. Each year, the river took away bits of rock and sand. Big winds took away bits of rock and sand too. Each winter, ice broke off chunks of rock.

This happened year after year. It is still happening. These forces of nature are called weathering.

Erosion is another force of nature. You can see erosion after a big rainstorm.

The rainwater rushes fast. It takes soil and small rocks with it. It can take bushes and trees too.

Forces of nature act slowly. They make small changes over years and years. But they never, ever stop.